A SHADOW OF MEMORIES

In praise

Tripti's contribution to society extends well beyond her professional life and even manifests through her writings.

Shri Trivendra Singh Rawat,
Chief Minister of Uttarakhand

TRIPTI BHATT

A SHADOW OF MEMORIES

RUPA

Published by
Rupa Publications India Pvt. Ltd 2019
7/16, Ansari Road, Daryaganj
New Delhi 110002

Sales Centres:
Allahabad Bengaluru Chennai
Hyderabad Jaipur Kathmandu
Kolkata Mumbai

Copyright © Tripti Bhatt 2019

This is a work of fiction. Names, characters, places and incidents are either the product of the author's imagination or are used fictitiously, and any resemblance to any actual persons, living or dead, events or locales is entirely coincidental.

All rights reserved.
No part of this publication may be reproduced, transmitted, or stored in a retrieval system, in any form or by any means, electronic, mechanical, photocopying, recording or otherwise, without the prior permission of the publisher.

ISBN: 978-93-5333-323-2

First impression 2019

10 9 8 7 6 5 4 3 2 1

The moral right of the author has been asserted.

Printed at Nutech Print Services, Faridabad

This book is sold subject to the condition that it shall not, by way of trade or otherwise, be lent, resold, hired out, or otherwise circulated, without the publisher's prior consent, in any form of binding or cover other than that in which it is published.

To my grandparents

Contents

Preface	ix
Little Touch	1
Identity Crisis	3
Revelation	6
Reincarnation	9
Afghanistan	10
Dialogue	13
Being Good	14
Getting Old	20
Choice	22
Song of Eternity	23
Sunshine	26
Achievement	28
Letter of Love	30
Saving Life	33
Paintings of God	35
Sorrow	37
Disillusionment Trilogy	38
I Water	38
II Fire	39
III Flowerpot (Earth)	40
Tribute	42
Family Tree	45
Inconsequential	47
Blue	49
Dusk	50
Prison Break	52
Eternity	53
Border	57
Departure	59
Tale of a Tree	61
Karma	63
A Learner's Dilemma	64
If I Die Today	67
Birth of Time	69
Amidst War	71
Before We Leave	74
Urban Flower	77
Panchtatva	79
Nostalgia	80
Wisdom	82
Nomad	87
Aftermath	92
Fate	95
Viciousness	96
Tonight I'll Smile	97
And I Am Empty Again	99
Let me...	101
Importance	103
Dichotomy	105
Hometown	110
Frozen Trilogy	112
I. Frozen	112

II. Bland	112	Imperfect	146
III. The Corpse	114	Pact	148
Meeting	115	Peace	149
Tsunami	117	If You Ever Love	150
Déjà Vu	121	Healer	152
To Thy Beloved	122	Book of Life	153
Escape	126	Conversation	155
Almost	127	Scribbling	157
Camouflage	128	Prisoner of Dark	158
Ghosts	130	Everlasting	160
Seasons	131	Struggle	161
The Bird	132	Time	162
Spying Clouds	134	A Shadow of Memories	164
Death... Almost	135	Not Beautiful	166
Obituary	136	Reader	168
Farewell to Youth	137	Euthanasia	169
God on a Beach	139	Acidic	171
Survival	142	Forever	173
Merchant of Dreams	143	River in Moonlight	175

Preface

Poetry has the burden of an overwhelming surge of emotions, even if recollected in tranquillity, and the burden must unburden the reader of the realities of his own world and reproduce even if partially, pictures vivid and powerful; meanings hidden or forgotten—a universe to be immersed into as a respite from the mundane. In complete realization of the demands of form and content in a genre assimilating artistic refinement and literary responsibility, I have attempted to put forth an assortment of poems that I have relished writing since childhood.

With an undercurrent of temporariness or loss, in this collection of poems I have tried to touch territories uncomfortable or dark, while not losing track of the shades of love and an inherent eternity imparting meaning to an otherwise meandering fragile quest called life.

> Don't love me like the world does
> For the roses wither too soon

> The fires quench too quickly
> The castles prefer to ruin.
>
> —'Merchant of Dreams'

Any creation has to survive the scrutiny of time more than that of any eye and must be true not only to the spirit of its times but also to the times ahead as a footprint of contemporary truths. Poetry in particular must also impart a feeling of beauty even if in melancholy, be able to convey a sense or at least a sensibility, provoke uncomfortable questions or attempt to answer a few in its abstractions, be able to play with imagination while delving into reflections much deeper than the realm of words.

While one can't downplay the role of experiences in impacting one's thought process, more often than not the muse for my poems has emerged in an unanticipated moment, giving shape to empathy, contemplations and perceptions. I can give no better example than the poem inspired from a glorious 1972-photo of Richard Nixon in China, on which I fixed my gaze and ended up immediately penning down a poem, a few lines of which read as:

> What is but a moment
> If not frozen for eternity

> What is but an image
> If it was all it could ever be.
>
> —'Revelation'

Poems like 'Sunshine', 'Revelation', 'Blue', 'Birth of Time', among others, touch the creative aspect of destruction. The lens of temporariness doesn't mar the vigour or delicate pleasures and poems like 'Letter of Love', 'Tribute', 'River in Moonlight, 'Afghanistan' are a testimony to this fact. The poem titled 'Identity Crisis' is about lost love as much as about the person choosing it in a very deep sense of duty. Poems like 'Dusk', 'Border' and 'Wisdom' throw one into a contemplative mood while there are ones with melancholy hues including 'Obituary', 'Ghosts', 'Sorrow'.

Language has its own limitations and more often than not it falls short of truly expressing what the soul experiences. The complex interplay of infinite shades of pain, pleasure or an absence of both cannot be bound or limited in words, it might even end up losing the original intensity of feelings and this is the dilemma and challenge for a poet. The restless attempt to let bloom what cannot be expressed through words is beautifully portrayed in a few lines:

The mere thought
Of my dear
Writing to you
Has sadly burnt
In the ruthless flames
Of what I am.

—'Letter of Love'

Or

These shapes on paper
Thinking of you
Like painting a fragrance
Touching a sound
They can't be true.

—'Tribute'

The span of these works spreads across many years hence it must not come as a surprise that the style and metre lack consistency; also the simplicity of language I realize is a slippery slope, on the one hand leaving room for allegations, at times even wrath of critics, for sounding trivial while simultaneously attracting relatability and unadulterated pleasure of comprehension.

Your eyes remind me of childhood
You smell to me like home.

—'Nostalgia'

It is my firm belief that innovation, craft or flamboyance must not be at the cost of connection that poetry develops or even at the cost of an intensity in plain crudeness. There is again a culpability of both overt objectivity and over abstraction and on this double-edged sword a poet carefully treads.

> I know the sun is shining
> Every day in disguise
> They think the night has fallen
> I know you've closed your eyes.
>
> —'Let Me...'

Having faith in the ordinariness of all unusual and uniqueness of all ordinary, I think that seemingly simple experiences of day-to-day life can also have profound impact on our worldview and a view of our inner self. A swipe or deletion for example is a gesture that can penetrate much deeper than what reaches our eyes...

> Trying to remember
> Who I was
> Before I erased myself
> From your words
> In my phone.
>
> —'Scribbling'

It's in various shades that memories manifest themselves and shape us. The interwoven flavours of nostalgia I wish would appeal to influence the minds of all age groups.

> Pink evenings of my time
> And talks from a heart to a heart
> An island of knowing and being known
> In a world falling apart.
>
> —'Dusk'

My poetry would have served a purpose if it can inspire one to spare a moment to think amidst the cacophony or mundane vulgarity of our ordinary lives and shrug off a part of the settled dust. It is in absolute realization of inherent flaws and imperfections of all art and abstract that I put forth this work before readers and in audacious hopes of an elusive forever, sincerely hope that it will be relished.

Forever is ultimately, just a beautiful day!

Little Touch

Little things
Little lives
Die on the
Carpet of great.

Snubbed, scoffed
Some wither
As a careless
Carving of fate!

Little thoughts
Little drops
Flow like
A song on dew.

Great things
Mighty and cruel
Burn them
In hope of new!

Passion, creation
Wandering soul
Search for a
Shelter unarmed.

The little, the pure
Muse, mistress
For the world
To be charmed!

Identity Crisis

Am I the one who watches
Love walking by time's side
With a queer charm and halo
Rising and falling as tide.

White as snow, pure as blood
Charting its ritual course
Unaware of yester's yearnings
Unaware of yester's mores.

Or am I the mystic
Preaching the truths of love
Burning my own desires
And passions in failure's stove.

Taming for the world
Storms, winds, breeze
Killing the meek romances
Making fires freeze.

Or am I the loner
Quietly waiting for love
Scribbling beneath my shadows
Putting bricks above.

Glancing at the galleries
Where glorious marches are on
Sighing, praising, blooming
Back to my groove am gone.

Or maybe I am a flower
In heavenly garden of God
For love I wait to pluck me
Smell me dead and applaud.

My eyes are open to wilderness
My roots are destined in dark
My arms in heavenly swaying
But I, the cursed monarch.

Am I the splendid morning
Compared to a beauty's eyes
Hiding the love when it wants to
Climb on a cloud in disguise.

On the white it perches
And shines as a pearl black deep
It flies to faraway places
But to vanity weep.

Or maybe I am the giant
Mundane shapeless rock
Knows not touch and tenderness
Knows not love nor talk.

Dazed at miseries like weeds
Growing on the love's weak soil
Proud at my strength and choices
The plot of love I foil.

But who knows if I am a piper
Engrossed in melancholy tunes
Love follows me madly
I drown it into the ruins.

In thy eyes am a butcher
Chopping the butterfly's wings
But I quietly obey my love
It wants to die I sing!

Revelation

What is but a moment
If not frozen for eternity
What is but an image
If it was all it could ever be.

Walking through silent nights
Frozen thoughts, flowing water
Words breaking boundaries
As a fountain
Alas! A river it could not be.

To be amazed at the glories of man
The ravishing force of nature
Or if nothing, my soul
Had to be verified
By enchantments divine
As the smoke from these chimneys
Destined to walk high
A cloud of water or beauty
It could never be.

To see, listen, feel
Shed tears at the miseries around
But pass as a deep breath
In cacophonies
Unseen, unheard, unfelt
Unnoticed, uncared for
I exist and make them alive
Their God I could never be.

The paths I tread
Neither different nor glorious
Never distantly anything that shines
Parched land, dry leaves, lone evenings
Dying men like cattle
These yearnings of my heart
In this graveyard of insignificant memories
I had no flower to keep at thy lips
No words of love
No sighs of passion
No stories of brutal wars
For my grandchildren
Perhaps I am a man
Who could not be.

My days are sprinkled
With finest of moments

My thoughts have a grandeur
Above all passions
I can see beyond the mundane
I can paint all the colours of pain
But what is but a moment
If not frozen for eternity
What is but an image
If it was all it could ever be.

Reincarnation

Memories are never killed
They are buried alive
They rise
As a vine of grapes
In the winters of your life
They rise as creepers do
And reach almost your heart
As a penance they
Change their course
And you crave
To taste their wrath.

Afghanistan

Will you wait for me to return?
Dipped in honey
Soaked in evening sun
Standing tall, proud
An island of serenity
In chaos and crowd
Oh darling!
I wonder if I ever
Will live this moment
This bliss again
On a swinging thread
I lay my pain
The carpets of mirror
Die for you
To tread them
Hermits sing
Your chants
And I want
To embrace you
As the air

Before I leave heavily
Without knowing
Will you be the same?
If ever I return,
Will I want you to be
There for my sojourn?
Will ever I want
You to be as you are?
Will ever I exist
Once I am so far?
Will you ever resist
The seasons of autumn and spring?
Will you hold the pieces
That a time will bring?
Millions of questions
So deep
As I glide through the night
Dark is the sky
Uncertain my flight
A creature of craft
I spread my strong wings
Not afraid to burn
Just curiously wonder

Will you ever
Wait for me to return?
Dipped in honey
Soaked in evening sun.

Dialogue

We will talk one day
Long after we declare
The God of words
To be angry forever
Long before silence sleeps
Forever between the lines.

We will talk the day, the smell
Of tears emerges from wet earth
And pearls of truth
Shine on bed of heart.

We will talk of blood and death
The dark remains of pain
All that was hidden beneath
The layers of solitude.

We will talk acknowledging efforts
Caressing faults
We will talk as we grow old
'Dear destiny'!

Being Good

A good girl
Covers her body
Carefully as a sin
Lest a pervert gets aroused.

She must not step out late
Must not drink
Must not talk
With too many boys
Must not appear
Too loud
Or too soft.

She must choose
The moral times
Lengths and words
For all her thoughts.

A good girl
Never makes love
Nor does she

Talk about sex, nudity
Or eccentric arts
She must not try
To touch excellence
In territories
Beyond a clean room
Good food
And a desirable body.

A good girl has beauty
But not uncomfortably high
Has brain too
But not bigger than her peers.

A good girl
Believes in all gods
Of heaven and this world
Creates some as well
Whenever time demands
She must never question
Demand or dictate.

A good girl
Should submit, succumb
Ask plead or beg
Or simply wait

For a magnanimous heart
To have pity
Or lust on her.

A good girl
Accepts and sacrifices
She never goes to police
If she is raped.

How can she?
She is the torchbearer
Of dignity
Of her family
Clan, caste, religion
A torchbearer
Of godliness
Purity.

There are higher truths
Than her own
Miniscule existence
A good girl
Knows that.

She does not believe
In truths

Other than taught to her
Ever since
She could learn.

She does not
Doubt authority
Nor does she fight
For anything
From crayons
To human rights.

She always forgives
Always forgets
Always watches
As someone treads
Over her body
Mind and soul.

She must be happy
In whatever happens
She must adapt
To indifference about
Anything beyond
Her market value.

A good girl is fluid
Just like her tears
To fit flawlessly
Into all roles assigned.

It's her obligation
To be perfect and silent
Or else become
The default reason
For all the
Woes of the universe.

A good girl exists
Within all girls
And we quietly feed
Or starve her
Even live
An uncomfortable duality
Switching between
The good and the bad.

Some of us kill her too
But not in a proud defiance
Rather in sheer
Accidents of destiny
That nonetheless spawn

Even more commandments
More examples
More reasons
For the future good girls
To remain good.

I am tired of this game
I close my eyes
And dream
Of a world
Where being good
Has nothing to do
With being a girl.

Getting Old

When you wanted something to stay
As it flew over
Like a paper plane
Heavily it carried a fragrance along
For which you stood and wept for long.

When you wanted something to stay
On the surface as a scar
It felt the pain chosen
Healed, tore itself apart
And you wept for a missing part.

When you wanted something to stay
In the silent pond of care
It grew limbs and swam
To shores distant and blue
And you wept as if you knew.

When you wanted something to stay
For a wild journey afar
Feeling harmony

Waiting for paths to be chart
And you wept for a false start.

When you wanted something to stay
As a memory at least
In pastures of heart
And you wept when it vanished
Before even it was...

Choice

What is more cruel
To be done with untruth?
Feed it to your soul
Let you dwell in illusions?
Make it bloom,
Let you try to fly
On feathers inexistent?

Or to kill it ruthlessly
Unshackle you
Of this envelope
Shorten your path
To realizations
But starve you
Of promises
Beauty of hopes.

Song of Eternity

If I be a song
Which song would it be?
That what quivers
On the boundary
Of your lips and mine
Or that lingers
In the old sea shores
Silent far behind.

The song that plays
In the dead of night
In the drops
Sliding swiftly
Through branches of might.

Or the melody divine
That existed in anxiety
Before the commission
Of sins
And the birth
Of death and desires.

What song shall I be
To remain in all fires
The music
Unlike life
Not to float or be forgotten.

What song what grace
Shall it be if it were?
Perhaps not of passion
Too temporary
Not love; too deceptive
Not pain; too loathed
Not the least of gods
It's sham.

What song shall I be
Of what gardens
Not of heaven
Or the riches of earth.

The song that I be
Is growing
Not towards the world
Nor light
Not for an applaud
Or insight.

Piercing deep
As roots of cactus
And I wonder
Why the spines dance
But not to be seen
Music wanders
In the expanses
Shivering faintly
Surviving
Despite everything
Strong, firm, mundane
Hidden, deep, insane
A music, a melody
A life too deep
Hidden in and for
The sand of time.

Sunshine

Memories
Do not wash me over
As the first sun ray
Of a quiet morning
Nor do they sink
Heavily beyond horizon
As I wish them to
So often.

I feel the photons
Packet by packet
Hitting me
Hard
I feel the waves
Encircling me
Like a flowing ribbon
Maybe a rainbow
Which deceptively
Tries to strangulate
So often.

Despite all
I realize
Memories
Nonetheless
Have created
Perhaps unwillingly
The life in me
The light in me.

Achievement

Many breeze of dreamy youth
And storms of strong passions
Passed through these towering gates
Today are new coronations.

These celestial celebrations
Of temporariness
Fragrances that die overnight
Feelings that fade like vapour
Roads that bury your flight.

A stoic air of wisdom
Surrounds it all
A halt, old gaze, silence
Ripe showers
Drenching a budding withdrawal.

I look as unhurt as I could
As the ashes
Of beloved days that once

Clinged to my skin
Are washed away too far.

As a habit I wave my shoots
Of the visible existence
As not to defy or offend
This cycle of perpetual meaninglessness
Burying my roots in the meantime
Deeper in the dark.

We all are drunk and mad and happy
We understand and praise
Glossy coverings
Over the skeletons of truths

This is my dear
A day to raise a toast
And celebrate
Before this carnival dissolves
Once again
Into nothingness.

Letter of Love

Where shall I write
A letter of love?

On something as fragile
And inconsequential
As a remnant of dead tree?
Trusting something
So clever as words?

I would belittle pain
If blood is what I write with
And betray feelings
If I constrain them
In a cage of thoughts.

How do I write of love?
If at all it can withstand
The span, depth, weight
Of existence
Dripped in transient shades
And survive

The fatal thorns
That it is destined
To be wrapped with.

Or I wonder
Should I at all
Attempt to define
And thus defy
The universe of universe
That undergoes
Explosions
Expansions
Every fraction of a fraction
Of a moment?

How do I pour
The molten stars
The ferocious storms
That I witness underneath
A calm surface?

The volcanoes
Too vehement
To be withstood.

Which kind of love is it
To be written about?
And letter did I say
To contain
The fissions
Of ferocious feelings.

The mere thought
Of my dear
Writing to you
Has sadly burnt
In the ruthless flames
Of what I am.

Saving Life

The ugly dry tree
On the verge of death
Looked hopefully above
And peeped
Across the sheet
Of clouds
To ensure
It's allowed to die
Peacefully this time
No raindrop is thrown
Abrupt, unwanted
As oxygen to a dying man
Pulling him back
To hell.

He has always hated men
And the concept
Of saving
An otherwise
Swift walk to unshackle
These roots unwarranted.

As he waited
For it to not rain
His old wisdom announced
The fire in deep forests
It must be the two trees
Turned to stone
Out of contempt
They must have again
Clashed against each other
After a hard day
Mercy oh lord!
And may it reach me soon.

Mumbled the log
Rain rushed suddenly
And the nurse too
With an oxygen mask
In a distant ICU
Many lives were saved today.

Paintings of God

As a distant ship
Kisses the horizon
Soaks in waters deep
Separating, uniting
Redefining
An illusion of separation
Whisper the skies and seas
'Tis all but one
Ever encompassing
Vastness.

Shades and shadows
In you and me
You glide float
Drink breathe
All but parts of me
The flames glow
As ember at night
And some scribbling
Becomes trees.

My innocence
Wants to laugh at
Kiss and drink
This oneness
Float and swim and fly
Across the water
And sky
Chew crush
Blow or meddle
All the ships to nowhere
Erase and applaud
To myself as I recreate
New shapes
New wonders
Ever aware, ever ignorant
As I redraw
An illusion of separation
In my canvas.

Sorrow

I have a contract with sorrow...
We do not acknowledge
Each other's presence
Within ourselves
We never appear together in public
Nor do reveal
The secrets of our intense
Inseparability
We have our mistresses
Of joy, beautiful
And we feel jealous
And betrayed
Yet live a parallel life
Of stolen truths
Not for display
Finding solace
Away from this brutal
Chaos of world
Only in each other's arms.

Disillusionment Trilogy

I Water

I thought I was the desert
And you, the alluring rain
I missed you and the dry sands
Were jealous of the distant lands.

I waited for eternity
For prayers to be answered
Dusk to dawn, dawn to dusk
The wisdom of heavens I pondered.

I thought I was the desert
Miserable lonely patch
The heat of my heart sought but you
It had to be holy water.

My penance, salvation, divinity, me
All I thought resided in you
Today it rained they say good lord.

While I sigh
Amidst these torrents
Washed, Devastated.

II Fire

I thought I was doomed
A being to be
Baked in the embers of life.

I caught fire one day
And my sins
Flamed with all their might
I wanted to be consumed.

Burning day and night
The smoke was charred
With half burnt soul
I became fire
And craved for you,
With fiercest of my fervour
And hunger and might.

You loved me but once
That one dark moonlit
Fateful winter night
When I discovered, my darling
You were...
A firefly.

III Flowerpot (Earth)

I thought I was the earth
I searched for seeds in me
Confided, struggling hard
Until free
To pierce my existence
Bloom to the heavens...

I thought my
Dead nerves
Might come to life one day
I wanted to feel anything
Get soaked
And suddenly I did
But only to come to terms
That I am not
The earth anymore.

Nothing ever sprouted
Of the pain
Today my reflections
Haunt me
In a sinful shape
As I behold
Dead flowers of mother earth.

Tribute

These shapes on paper
Thinking of you
Like painting a fragrance
Touching a sound
They can't be true
Still my dear
I write of you.

A moment
Being carved
All music in place
The stars of twilight
And the night they chase
All stand waiting
Perhaps for you
And like a melody
I write of you.

A painted postcard
Was abandoned today
Carefully holding

A mysterious hue
I should keep it safe
With all of its mates
The address unknown
Till we find the new
In the meantime
Let's keep painting blue
As a pious ritual
I write to you.

With all my limits
And flaws, manners
Writing it small
Never had any banners
Somewhere someday
In an old storehouse
Or in the thatches
Housing old cows
An unfashionable
Book will be found
Some soul in love
Will hear its sound
Some flower of desert
Will get a drop of dew
Some lost ship
Will find its crew

In hope of that day
For a love of that time
I am keeping an imperfect
But art sublime.

It had to be my cravings
Sheltered in this moment
A sigh wrapped in words
But nothing to lament
This song of solitude
Of a hermit isn't new
Someday it will find
A companion true

Till then we part
And safe inside words
I keep a piece of you
In these shapes on paper
Between false and true
An image I seek
My dear it's you.

Family Tree

Like birds we perched
Together that day
Like birds we flew
Afar and stray
Like wind
We existed
Never to accept
We were there
Like seeds
We waited
To be tested.

Of leaves we saw
The destiny
Of love
Too much they clinged
Fell to death
Facing above
Together we were
Insistent apart
Denying we loved

Denying we crave
Denying we belong
To the same soil
Same labour pains
Of the ripe old fruits.

Tales of glory, toil
The green leaves
The dead leaves
The twigs
All generations
Loved
Each of us
And we loved still
All those departed
Never to return.

We must fly back today
And between
The new buds
Quietly make
A nest of dead twigs
On the same old branch
Of the same old tree
It is after all
A festival today.

Inconsequential

How is it
To be forgotten
Sink deep
Inside records?

Gulping
As you die
The chilling
Salty waters.

Insatiable thirst
Of thoughts
Unquestionable
Surrender to gods
How is it to immerse
In an abandoned cry?

How is it
To be forgotten
And find
Treasures ever alluding

Mocking
As you sigh?

The grinning
Lonely expanses
Sadistic charm
Of trapping
Unconquerable thunder
Unarmed, unapplauded
As you quietly try.

How is it
To be forgotten
Sinking, dying
Surrendering
Finding, fighting
Conquering?

Defeated
Or proud
Trenches
Or cloud
But ever unwitnessed.

Unwritten
Unchallenged
Unthought
Undead.

Blue

I thought I was alone
As I counted the endless waves
Stood confronting
The deep blue mountains
Drew patterns
On clouds in azure sky
Weaved my dreams
As blue petals in midnight
Sank inside myself
Into the deep blue waters.

It suddenly appeared
You have always
Been there
You have always
Revealed
You have always had answers
Always confided
Always won
And always
Created me
Out of the blue!

Dusk

Pink evenings of my time
And talks from a heart to a heart
An island of knowing and being known
In a world falling apart.

Mighty rivers of light
Below the bridge I'd lean on
Smiles and whispers conveyed untouched
Noises unheard unknown.

The hurry together to nowhere
Clicking the souvenirs of nothing
Conundrum of silence and words
To be solved perhaps still waiting.

Pink evenings of my time
I'll miss them when I am old
May the stories grow prettier
To be lived, to be told.

The purple the grey the fiery
I've tasted the shades all known
But something within an evening
Talks in a deep dark tone.

Some answers the eyes reveal
When it's not a day or night
Some shades of a soul you see
Between the red and white.

It's something about an evening
Which is so much like me
I am but still I am not
It may or may not be.

Prison Break

A dent in the universe
Was all she was told
She could, if ever, create
Nonchalantly
Being crushed, she persisted
Hitting the walls
Of this undented prison.

They thought
The game is finished
But instead
The pieces
Flew away as a debris
Of billions of aspiring dents
To break a new prison.

Eternity

A river flows
In every universe
Carrying the
Fragrance of songs.

It flows through
The marshes of mind
Meandering through
Being found and lost.

Trying to live
Trying to drown
Trying to forgive, it flows
To another universe.

Breaks the rocks
Of judgement
Dissolves the barriers
Of morality.

Crushing and carving
It moves
And I bid goodbye
To an era
Enveloping an
Ill-fated existence.

I watch as it flows
Realize as it grows
From a river
To a story.

How it has lived
Across time
Across tales
And how I have yearned
In all these times.

How in every universe
A part of me
Has drunk the waters.

How in every life
I have wanted
To die like this.

How in every sky
My song has echoed.

How in every wandering
I have found myself always.

How in every course
This river has lived in me.

How through all the stories
I have lived in this river.

I look at the sky
As it flows away
To some heaven
I wait for the monsoon morning
For it to embrace me afresh.

I wish all stories are
Weaved and washed
Hidden in drops
Shine in bright colours
Dry in magnificent sun
Soaked back in pieces
And river flows again.

Till that day
I wait for my turn
I live in this universe
Understanding
What I can.

I see gods conceal
The forbidden
I see my river,
Living despite me...
Every night
From every universe
Stealthily,
Heavens talk to me.

Border

There is a fire
That floats in me
There is a fire in you
Both of us burn
In similar sins
Keeping the flames
Alive and true.

The hour of death
Seems not so far
The day of judgement
Awaits us all.

The fire of reason
Hate, obsession
Of cause, of love
Of power, of gods
All kill, all die
All lay bare
Exhausted, charred
All turn to ashes.

At the end of it all

We look into the fire
With knowledge
With guilt
And leave it
To open seas within

We sigh, we row
Tirelessly
We save the flames
To kill us one day
In all our honour
And glory

We won't quench it
Nor let the other do
We will burn down
Everything and everyone
Generation after generation

And as always
The fire will win
Inherited perpetually
Each side.

Departure

How did we depart?
What kept us away?
What was 'tween the sighs
What lived beyond that day?

How was it that you left
Unceremoniously, or was it me?
As if the wind steals
A leaf off a winter tree.

Perhaps we departed
As endless waves of a lonely shore
To arrive, touch, elate and wet
Never to be there
Ever as before.

Was it a stone you threw
That rests in trenches of my heart?
Or I threw one vaguely
But which shattered thou art.

What unsettles so deeply
When ages have passed
Which departure is permanent?
Which ritual of reunion barred?

How did we depart?
How does it matter today?
It was just an umbilical cord
That broke and kept us apart, away.

Tale of a Tree

Time when a leaf
Pierced by the winds
Reminded of itself
Decides to fall down
In a desire to flow
With the freezing currents.

Time when a bird
Reminded by the winds
Pierced by itself
Decides to fly up
With a hope to glide
In the cruel sky.

Time of life
Freeing oneself from
Warm pleasures of
Togetherness
To embrace the unknown
Piece by piece
In a storm.

I become the leaf
And the bird
At once
A part of me flies
A part of me floats
Breaking free
To uncertainty
In anticipation
Of discovering
Or being discovered
To be perhaps
Made into a shelter
For the fairy tales to live.

Karma

It's loss and pain
That maketh a man.

A conscience that weeps
On what the world reaps.

A desire that burns
Against all what it earns.

For all unkilled and all unborn
And all the pieces of soul that's torn.

I wish I was given a game again
I wish I was not made a man.

A Learner's Dilemma

Smell of songs
They sang to me
Touch of the words
That floated in glee.

The air, the woods
Jewel embedded sky
The eyes, the tears
And alas that sigh!

The frozen time
The static rivers
Hope deep inside
That goodness delivers.

To live in that moment
To breathe in that air

I give you all my passions
My joys and despair.

To taste the nectar
Of flowers divine.
To gaze at the riot
Of colours sublime.

To set free my soul
In waves invisible
To listen to the stories
Of rocks sand and gravel.

To fly with burdens
And sink with clouds
To play all alone
And hide in the crowds.

To walk on water
And drown in a smile
To wait for nothing
And rush for the trial.

To wake up in dreams
And sleep in chaos
To live in the sunshine
Where darkness glows.

To tie up my thoughts
In freedom and pride
And throw out judgements
For the world to decide.

To save the treasure of silence
Hidden lonely and deep
Spread words in the air
For you to smell and read.

To tread the lonely roads
To talk to the lost sky
I come to thee to know me
I want to give it a try.

If I Die Today

At times I feel
If I die today
I'll walk away
With much unsaid.

The storms of the times
They say were naive
The echoes the yearnings
The ghosts and the graves.

The ripples on the stones
The thaws of the oceans
The frozen galleries
Of heart all molten.

I have the stories—
The towering trees
Engulfed in a shell
Lying abandoned
On the floor of my heart.

They refuse to grow
And today I bow
I agree to my fate
Soil I am, for soil I wait.

To come to me again
Lend me its arms
To bury the remnants
Of times, of charms.

The remnants of pain
The remnants of dreams
All that I have
All that seems.

Stories time wrote
On the slate of my soul
Will emerge again
Will be buried again.

If I die today
I do realize
Time has hidden
Truths to be told
Peep in eyes of eternity
And it shall unfold.

Birth of Time

In a moment of moment's birth
When timeless stories are told
A moment asks another
What can a moment behold?

The flight of my dreams
To lands afar
Mischievous secrets
Rooted in my heart.

The moment itself
And the moments yet to come
One in all
And all in one.

The moment beholds
The secret of time
And holds itself
Against siege divine.

It flies it drowns
In search of itself
Wants to reborn
Before it's gone.

The life of a moment.
Resides in another
And passes as silence
To the child from mother.

In the moment within
The moment beholds
The moment of death
Or perhaps.

In the moment within
The moment beholds
The key, to eternity.

Amidst War

If at all you do
Do you see the colour of my pain?

Lingering in the vast skies
Still in a heavy chain
The shades of thoughts
The winds of love
And depths condemned to be trained.

The hope of glory
If at all it is
In a life so short and vain
Talk in all your truth
Do you see the colour of my pain?

Yearnings of heart
New paths to chart
All lost in a frame so fixed
The bird of life
The soul of a wanderer
All miserably tricked

The gushing rushes of my blood
I'd love to shed always
But in a passion
Which is my own
And for the reasons
I choose to be known

Alas! The sounding bugle
Reminds it's time again
I look into your eyes to find
If you see the colour of my pain.

The marches are perfect in order
A harmony I lost from my heart
It's all chaos and dreams within
But rules are here to take charge
My smile, tears, agony, fears
My life, my story
Of ladder to the stars
They are all to be wrapped
And locked unfed
It's a world of arms and bars.

I feel the river of time
Drenching me flowing afar

Some splashes contained a fire
Some destined to freeze as a star
May be the rainbow of life
Is visible at your end
Maybe the deep black lakes
Reflect it and contain
Maybe you sigh and wonder?
Indeed it's the colour of pain.

Before We Leave

The pretence of existence
The pretence it did not.

The fables that were said
Unsaid that was.

The times that flew
And the ones which did not.

The memories I have
And ones you got.

The wind that blew
The soul that sighed.

All that I had
And all I denied.

The mornings without sun
The nights undone.

The days so dry
And talks all shy.

The silence, the talks
The moon, the walks.

The flowers of spring
And your heart, like a swing.

The games with a roar
And stillness of my door.

The reasons to laugh
The reasons to cry.

The glances which were
And the ones passed by.

The songs of the trees
The birds who would cry.

The roads with the bends
Those prints on the sands.

And the wind that blew
The soul that sighed.

And all that I had
And all I denied.

I am packing my bags
It's so much of all.

What should I keep?
What should I leave?

Urban Flower

When darkness wraps its gloomy veil
Over the wretched skies
Tormented arms and legs
Drag back to a home but exile.

Drudgery dirt and shattered hopes
Burdens of unfulfilled promises
All flock to their nests and cry.

Stars peep out in apprehension
And smile a shrewd smile
As all look for a gentle breeze
But find a hot wind vile.

Many eyes surrender
To the cloaks of destiny
Some close while some try.

The sweat the puffs
Suffocation the dust
And crawling lives in dismay

I walk briskly past this mayhem
Beyond the brooding for day.

Snaky paths crawling and slippery
Deceptive elusive ethereal
I walk it walk for you and walk
My dreams so dark yet real.

Noises are fading afar
Grip of night so intense
Pangs of pain persistent
Lost in your holy incense.

Monstrous shadows
Dreary nights
Fearsome paths
But I walk with life

I know you'll be there
Despite realities stark
White pure and fragrant
My flower that blooms in dark.

Panchtatva

Fire from your lips
Earth deep in your voice
Water from the pores
Dampness in your eyes
The breeze that fiddles
With your waving hair
And the warm embrace
Vast as seven skies
Today I found the elements
They say that make a man...

Nostalgia

Your eyes remind me of childhood
You smell to me like home.

In fleeting glimpses
Burdening days
Tired mind gets solace
In winds warm
Wrapped in love
Some parched some torn
But always
Straight from home.

As we laugh together
Youthful days
Quietly enter the room
At you they gaze.
I pluck a fruit of memory
Stealing a feeling uncertain
It tastes of my childhood
And it tastes to you the same.

Piercing the fluttering carpets
Surveying the islands of wool
The racing bundles of fire
The lightening, thunder
And now the grey old
Tired stacks of water.

But the showers
Still wet the earth alike
The golden mammoths
Born, live, die every day
Getting a new childhood
New years of impatient love.

They grow old every day
Tired, dejected, bleeding
Quietly caressing the scars
With you they decide
It's time to be born
As the door opens
Some wild flowers bloom
You smell to me like home...

Wisdom

What is a night of
Sorrow young man?
What is a night of joy?

Both equally deceptive of them
Both equally dark
Both insignificant
In a journey of million years
Both inflict deep scars.

What is a night of
Sorrow young man?

When you don't know
What to seek in light.
What battle you lose,
What sermon you forget?
When there was nothing
Worthwhile in sight.

This night, long may
Shall pass as they say
But the bigger question
Remains unanswered
What difference does it make
Without burden, without pain?

Where do you want
To reach in sunshine?

Which path at dawn
Do you plan to take?

This darkness you curse
This day this time
Perhaps because
The chariot of age
Hasn't marched far enough.

Perhaps you aren't cheated
By damsels of ecstasy.
Perhaps because wisdom
Matures in dark rooms
Dark times, dark ages
My boy.

What is a night of sorrow?
What is a night of joy?

Your follies and illusions
Wear a delusive blanket
And you sing merrily
As if forever.
You dance to your death
Or to death of your angels,
As the song
Ends abruptly
And you think it is
The dark night of joy.
The blanket one day,
Will burn my boy,
And the knives
Of disenchantment
Shall pierce your skin too deep
It will breed
But vices
Will feed false notions.

The night of joy
Is darker my boy
It is in this darkness
That the guardians

Of your demons
Carry you along
Unbaked in the heat of sorrow
Unknown to the cycles
Of day and night.

Admire it you will
In a greying beard
Fondly, in your lawn
Smoking a pipe
On a rocking chair
One old day
You'll be grateful my boy
To the sorrow's night.
It provokes the light
Flickering in you,
It flames the passions
Dying, dormant and cold,
It bleeds you to fuel
The lamps of day,
It challenges to jump
In abyss if you may.
The night of sorrow
Is cruel young man,
But cruel not enough
Not to fall in love.

Live it, keep a souvenir
Smell its fragrance
Deep in you.
Preserve it as a tender
Yellow flower wrapped in dew.
Press it neatly
In your guiding book,
As you walk away
From its dark embrace.
Tread your paths softly
Sing songs of hope
Bring rays of life
Let the night in you
Remain as a seed,
Let it remind
As it sprouts,
There always comes a day my boy
There always comes a day.

Nomad

Lost in the woods
A word from my soul
Lost as I am
In this game of withdrawal.

A flight, a journey
A road, a scar
A memory, a man
A dream too far.

What is my purpose?
Where do I dwell?
Where is my root?
Where is my smell?

Man of a man
I know I am
Your standards although
Trap me and damn.

Drifter I am
I'll leave very soon
This moment of existence
Your bane my boon.

I walk with my words
I fly with a sigh
I dance with desires
With time I die.

Then I am born
And I cry.

Before I give up
I choose to fly.

You can watch me in your world
A drama it is
I throw off this character
I deny the riches.

I am here I agree
But for a short while
To taste your life
To dwell in your style.

Wonder you may
At my strange denial
My terms are my own
My own is the trial.

I forget your ways
As soon as I look out
And see the sun shining
Or a sapling sprout.

My wings are huge
Invisible to thy eyes
I can't stay for long
There have been
A lot many sighs.

A magnet found me
In your world it lies
It keeps me with you
And I close my eyes.

A power to surrender
It gave to me
A charm in losing
And being with thee.

It hides me from the air
It loves me to my soul
It binds me to this world
It knows to control.

But in its heart
It knows I am a bird
It will flip one day
Repel me to my world.

The grandeur of this life
Impresses indeed
Time will however
Express my creed.

Words are waiting
To walk with me
My wings are heavy
I need to be free.

Before you soak them
In the rush of your tears
I need to flee
Fighting my fears.

Great were the times
Shimmering days
But not for long
Can they trap my grace.

A sip of free air
Is calling me again
I must leave now
The song is insane.

It's time to dissolve
In the air and fly
To dance with desire
To live before I die.

Aftermath

It rained
And washed away
A dusty day of life
It swept across gullies
Overflowing with filth.

I was walking
Knee deep
Struggling to figure out
The birth of that stream
Tirelessly I walked
Unending it seemed
I loathed it
Craving to get rid
I dragged myself
As it spread its kingdom
All over.

It then thundered
As if from within
A roar of disgust

And something dying
Crying for help.

It was amidst this battle
That it rained
And washed away
The dirty sides of life
I stand now abandoned
On the barren land
Of my mind
Swept away, flushed
Leaving nothing behind.

The water, the storms
I thought would unleash
The hidden to me
Never did I know
That all I ever possessed
Was but filth
And the gods of rain
Washed it all today
The storm is over
With nothing left behind

I, a naked destitute
Stand here enlightened
In the aftermath
Life was nothing
But a long dusty day.

Fate

The days of this glorious
Moon shall pass
And I wonder if you
Like the dead of this night
Would be pregnant with mysteries
Or rest in a random groove
Or flicker with flashes of vanity
Or glow as an ember's charm?

Or who knows
You'll stand tall
Unchanged, unperturbed
Like these solemn woods
Waiting for the night
To be conquered by sun.

Viciousness

I thought it would end
And give me a chance
I thought I would stay
And survive your glance
But this vicious
Circle of love
Throws me
Back to beginning always
And here I am
To succumb to your mysteries
Die before you
One more time.

Tonight I'll Smile

In the thoughts of
What is yet to come
Resonating with heart's
Unknown rhythm.

In the cloudiest of days
And stormiest of nights
I'll struggle, I'll march
Be true to my fights.

Then I'll flow
With the wave so high
I'll roar, I'll laugh
Victory will come by.

Giving it a warm welcome
Tonight I'll smile...

Remembering the children
Barefoot on ice
Their songs of joy
Those twinkling eyes.

Tonight I'll devote
A toast to their spirit
It's a time to explore
Possibility infinite.

I'll throw the pain
And face the world
Straight into its eyes
Tonight I'll smile.

And I Am Empty Again

I look into your eyes
And pour in my tears
When I can't hold
Stories untold
Any more.

Ball of fire sets by
With a heaviness inside
When it can't bake
The same mistake
Any more.

The prophecies come true
Times meet,
Birds die
When they can't fly
Any more.

Diamonds emerge in sky
With an emptiness inside
When they can't hide
Any more.

And I pour my tears
Deep into your eyes
When I can't hold
What cannot be told
Any more.

Let me...

I know the sun is shining
Every day in disguise
They think the night has fallen
I know you've closed your eyes.

Let me fill you heart
Before the emptiness can enter
Let me cure you just for once
One last time, just surrender.

Let me fill your eyes
With sweet dreams of summer
Let me show you the path
The light is getting dimmer.

I know you are afraid
Of the dark dull and grey
Hold my hands for once
And with me you pray.

Together we've done
And again we'll do
Believe in yourself
To it, be true.

Don't make the moon
Hide under the cover
The night is in a mayhem
Let's remove the clutter.

Afraid are your dreams
To speak out again
Hear your heartbeat
Sing a song insane.

You chose the glow of life
Through the darkest of ages
Let me fly and lift you along
Before your world crashes.

Don't break apart my love
You are my lost sunshine
Let me fill your heart
Just one last time.

Importance

You can be many things
Still be nothing
And no one
Lost like dreams
On sale in a market
Being shuffled
In and out
Layers and layers
Chosen and rejected
Again and again.

Meeting unknown people
Repeatedly in your dreams
And dreams being broken
Leading to a free fall
Caught midway
By mesh of
Yet another dream
So familiar
Yet so unknown
So oft repeated

But with the dread
Of similar unknown
Unauthentic
Untrusted.

Players of drama
And you doubt
If at all you are
Or just a fleeting glimpse
In some distant close eye
Slave to its desires
Tied to its schedule
Unknowingly.

Just an insignificant
Deja vu, a weird dream?
Where the unknown appearance
Claims to be something
More than a dream
Yet being tormented
Swinging in every sleep
From something to nothing
And back.

Dichotomy

I am a normal man
Born in a normal society
And by virtue of this
Fortune if I may so say
I must run
All my life
Towards something remarkable
Yet in ordinary ways.

I must do something
That makes me different
Yet in a prescribed manner
Something that sets me apart
Still keeps me in the herd
I must run in given directions
And at given speed
To remain accepted
By the ghosts of past
I must remember
I have to achieve
As a normal man

What the currents of time
Dictate me to.

Not to inherit
A war-torn nationality
Or drug addict parents
Or a slum to live in
Has filled me
With great responsibilities
I am supposed
To be normal.

After all I am
Not one of 'them'
I have to be therefore
One of 'us'
And carry the burden
Of comparisons
Benchmarks
For the rest of my life.

I must not complain
As a part of
Who I am
My passions must be trained
My eyes must not look
Too far, too low or too high.

My life must be
Programmed by perceptions
Not chosen
Not the least to be lived
But displayed
Compared
Weighed every moment
Against judgements of normalcy.

I have to dispose
My yearnings
And pack my normalities
In attractive packages
Paste a smiling face
Marching obediently
To places
Where normalcies converge.

I must flaunt all of it
Like everyone does
And laugh, cry, celebrate or kill
In a ritual manner
Like all normal men

I should keep changing

My wrappers
Lest I am thrown out
Of this honoured
Tradition of a herd.

My stories have died
Suffocating within these shells
I must bury, burn or forget them
Since stories are supposed
To be beautiful and moral
Even if we are not.

And they should be so
In a manner and to the degree
An unknown God
Of the normals decided.

I must hide shamefully
The high tides of melancholy
The hollowness of my heart
The beauty I wish
Be with me
The words in wind
That I used to paint my dreams...

No, no, no! I must return

And keep dancing
On the senseless tunes
With specified steps
After all it is
A day of celebration
And I belong to the creed
Of normal men.

Hometown

I think of you
Not on my way
When I struggle to live
To make it to the end
I think of you
At heights of proud glories
Peak of the summits
As I conquer
Trenches unfathomable
The wildest winds
When tamed by me.

I emerge alone
Victorious indeed
Beholding the fruits of joy
Defeating to death
An intense contender
Perhaps in me.

Fierce brutal, aggressive

Thirsty to win
Ready to die
And to throw
On its face
Whatever life demands
As a fuel.

But all of it,
Maybe more
Suddenly dissolves
In a thought of yours
And melts down
As a palace of ice
Majestic but nothing
Before a winter noon.

A careless stray cloud
Smitten by your sunset smile
Suddenly turns yellow.

In your romancing roads,
Blooms a bougainvillea
And drifting over this breeze
I surrender for life.

Frozen Trilogy

I. Frozen

The quest for life
Plays cruel games
Of hide, hide and hide
One never seeks, never receives
In the process, it turns out
What was supposed
To be with thee
Passed away quietly
While one was busy
Trying to preserve it
In a frozen nothingness.

II. Bland

No fire no sparks
Just a long road
And a smoky
Lonely afternoon

No promises to break
No place to reach out
I wish to feel; get rid
Of this vacuum
Numbness
Devoid of even pain
This long unbearable journey
Sans destination
To rest, reach or weep.

Rainbows
Hang in despair
Waiting to be hunted.

Tired, I'll walk
Let the winds talk
And wake me up
From this semi-conscious
World
Revive me
Shake deep inside
Till that happens
I'll keep walking
Alone to nowhere
Along this
Frozen
Nothingness.

III. The Corpse

I faced you yet again
Like every day I do
Ignored,
Walked briskly
Away from you
I know you are there
Talking to me
As usual
About your death
And how it refuses
To spare you
For the world.
How you fight
Every day, every moment
With your dead body
Ever preserved
In this frozen nothingness.

Meeting

Cloud of wax
To meet
Cloud of fire
Today
A bird has borrowed
Wings of desire
Today.

The cloud of wax
Hurriedly floats
It has to make a way
Fire slowly drips
Down the hills
Time is the hunter
Time is the prey.

Slowly the game proceeds
But seeps a cloud grey
Between the wax and fire
Between the water and sky.

I quietly pray
For the bird to reach
Where it belonged
As I witness
The vast sky of wax
Waiting for fire
To emerge from sea,
Waiting for clouds
To immerse in thee.

Tsunami

You splash in like a wave
On the shores of my mind
Return to thy abode
Just to remind
How empty the world is
How plain is the sky
How silent the voices
How lonely, I.

The scarlet hues of sunset
The glorious sea on the show
The chirping and hustling
The life in this ghetto
All in the moment
Wrapping your presence
As you walk back
It's all but pretence.

The wave strikes again
Customs renew
The laughter, frolics

The mounts to pursue
The baggage, burden
Hopes, wisdom
Revive, allure
Suddenly waves strike
Again on shore.

The sun is alive
So are my dreams
Both are red
Lost in streams
Both are distant
Still so close
Both prefer sinking
Amidst the chaos.

And here comes the wave
All gushing once again
And the sands are drenched
Alas! The poor game!
So similar in my mind
To be soaked, to be dried
To be found, to hide.

Tales that are written
Just to be washed
Are not my dreams
Neither the costs
This is the secret
In me it was
I play at my will
I create I kill
I am the hand
Imprinting the shape
I am the sand
Absorbing my fate
I am the wave
To come and destroy
Laugh and return
Release a new joy
Till I return
Again with my might
Till I rule
Again, till I fight.

The sun is the sacred
Guardian of my dreams
They lie in its heart
Colour is green.
Blood for sure

Is never the core.
Maybe a veil
An entrance to mazes
Or a red demon
That fathoms and gazes.
Whatever the mystery,
Let it confide
Let the sun shine
The sand be dried.

Déjà Vu

Roads that we tread
Return to us
Unharmed
Sounds that we whisper
Travel through spaces
Unarmed
Fragrances defy
The rules of destruction
And against all odds
Equally shocked
Alarmed
We meet, we talk
As if life is a dream
And pays us a visit
Once in a while.

To Thy Beloved

Memories slip swiftly
Down the sloping roofs
And my heart waits
For the next signs
Of greyness in sky.

Time swings
Back and forth
All in front of my eyes
The long bamboo oscillates
Waves to the time
And smiles at me reminding
I am not alone
Wandering between
Dilemmas of
Roots, wind and sky.

Brahmaputra casts spell
From a distance
As it swallows the fiery sun
Yet again

Sends an enchanting glance
Bypassing
The travellers of its surface.

I know it understands
Our shared agonies
All the tales
All the moments
Hidden in a quiet thatched roof
Soaked in rain.

It listens with its soul
The august song
Of a lonely fisherman
Warmth of this tea
Smell of my body
My soul, this mud
It knows it all.

It has the fire
Deep down protected
From coldness of this world
It meanders around
Engulfing me
In its paternal trust
I keep swaying

Like the bamboo shoots
I keep praying
To the goddess of desires.

But reflections
In this divine solitude
Make me realize
That I want
My songs
To remain unheard
My prayers unanswered
My fragrances to dissolve undetected.

I want this rain
To remain in me forever
And this sun to sink
Deep into my soul
I want today to drink
Brahmaputra
And all its shades
False and true.

I want the
Sloping roofs
To keep their stories
Safe with me

I want more reasons
To come back perhaps
To return what I absorbed
And absorb what I could not
From your soft wet arms
Guwahati...

Escape

I swam but to be caught
The currents I thought
Would throw me to shore
To kill me, or more
But to disgrace
Of ritual case
I waited to die
For death to deny
Respite or peace
I ended therefore
In eternal tease
Not to surrender
My secret creed
I could not weep
I could not stop
I swam always
But to be caught.

Almost

What happens
Flows,
In river of time.

What does not
Lies dead
As a rock.

What lies in-between
Amuses me,
The almost,
The yet to be,
The could,
That lives in me
Every moment
Yet, does not live fully
Lest it flows away.

Camouflage

I make you wear
An overcoat of trivia
Conceal your innocence
With layers of heavy masks.

I close your eyes
And paint eyelids like stone
To guard your dreams
From passers-by.

I arm you with nothingness
And send you
To trenches
Where millions of masks
Make a living.

I let you appear
Like one of them
Despite being torn
And burdened with guilt.

Then wait for you
To blossom again
In star-studded silence
Of a moonlit night.

I wait for you
To undress
And leave all shadows behind.

I know you will emerge
In an unanticipated moment
I know you'll survive
This systematic torment.

I believe in you
Because you have
Always believed in me.

I know you will quietly
Embrace me in your arms
And reveal
What must not be said.

You will sing the songs of life
Forgotten melodies of love
I know that despite everything
It's hard to kill you
My poem!

Ghosts

The ghosts of two moments
Broke into my dreams
Ragged, old, dust-laden, torn
Straight into my dreams.

The clustered rituals of everyday life
Left no space for them to breathe
Tired, starved, dead, still they managed
To reach at least my dreams.

I am wide awake since then
The questions haunt, hang and linger
First ghost in tears asked, will you forget me?
Second with hope, will you remember?

Seasons

When it's a winter
In the garden of my mind
I shed what remains
And stand frozen in time.

When it's a summer
I sing for the dead
Flowers dead weeds
All dead that was sublime.

When it's a time
For the flowers to bloom
My mind
Sends fragrances
To summer and winter
In hope of moving the cycle of fate.

Nothing has changed
In all these seasons
Now it must
Rain forever.

The Bird

A part of me
Feeds on solitude
And dies a brutal
Death unheard.

It rises from not
The ashes or bones
But from the sky
Of which it's the bird.

It flew away
To horizons fearful
Dripping the molten pain
But all through the years
When I thought it was dead
It flew back to me again.

I pampered it, fed a sumptuous meal
Of solitude, silence and stillness
I broke the bondages

Of worldly customs
And let it blossom to fullness.

I let it paint itself
Let it make a truce
In its fragile existence
It had the privilege to choose.

It has perched on me
Since ages
And left me stranded
Today unheard...

A branch is empty
Silence has spread
The wait is intense
But it is but a bird.

Spying Clouds

The hovering bunch of spies
Assume shapes precarious
They lie, cheat, defy, deform
Along with me, all the way nonetheless.

I gazed at the sky
In their universe I peeped
To find forgotten monsters
Flying limbs and amputee horses
Great wars and greater moments
Of mingling and dispersals.

I saw a man in making
Struggling in the womb
And the shadow fell
On a poor peasant's land.

Gates to heaven or hell
Slide with the rythm of sighs
You befool us beautifully
The hovering bunch of spies.

Death... Almost

They always prayed,
You do not speak
What they never
Wanted to hear.

But fate deceived
On a fearsome night,
A silence
Talked to a tear.

Obituary

If I put together
All I felt for you
In the deepest state of being,
The unsaid will be lost,
The glances let down.
If at all I try
To tie it
Into a form,
The smiles will cry
To find a space
In the sharp edges
Of pen, of time.
And tears will dry,
As they touch
The brutal pages of custom.
Those words will slide
Like in an assembly line,
And my reverence
Will be reduced
To just another obituary.

Farewell to Youth

How many flights
How many journeys
How many steps
Running afar.

How much laughter
How many stories
How many dark
Secrets of ours.

We lived that day
Cried together
We saw it all stranded
As we walked away.

We saw it coming
We had to depart

Hands slowly drifted
Frozen was heart.

How many scenes, rituals
Flash together
How many meals, songs
To cherish forever.

How many struggles, stories
How many losses, deep scars
How many sorry, regrets
How, I wish I wasn't far.

I look at the mirror
Search for my remnants
Am I forgotten?
Or all are?

God on a Beach

Playing with sand
And shells and masks
Making some worlds
Before they are washed
Carving what slips
Shaping what flows
Caressing softly
Before it goes
With another wave
To another shore
Leaving me enchanted
And amused as before
A twist of finger
A ruined civilization
Force de majeure

On whims of my children
A tragedy of carelessness
Mistakes and beauties
I swiftly create
Giant universes
Hills, trenches, gorges
A fistful and a thought
A kingdom overthrown
New order to sought.

Who knows however
If the world within
Is burning between the cycle
Of dissolving
Drifting
Who knows if they are riddled
Equally as me
On the purpose and meaning
If at all there be.

Who knows there is a creature
Making castles
In the microcosm
Or zillions of them
Waiting to be born

Who knows if they worship
My fingers' ridges
And another wave means
Millions of ages.
Maybe their scientists
Search for another life
Maybe they are murdered
For insulting my pride.

How do they matter?
Except to them
How do I matter?
Despite their world
We are all serendipity
Equally restless, equally afraid
Equally insignificant, misled
And I am, eureka!
An unwilling, confused
Misunderstood God.

Survival

After all these years
We have somehow
Survived in each other
Despite each other
Says the seasoned voice
Of fire in water
Of water in fire.

Merchant of Dreams

Don't love me like the world does
For the roses wither too soon
The fires quench too quickly
The castles prefer to ruin.

The trampled pathways to bliss
Old, exploited and tired
How can they allow my chariot
Carrying the dreams I hired?

This is an expensive market
Offering pride, joy, peace
Love is on the shelf too perhaps.
All broken, shattered, sold in piece.

A carnival of cruel business goes on
In land of big promise, small heart

A dreamer, a lover, I try my fortune
Deception, depravity is also an art.

I sell dreams to be planted alive
Grow to great proportions unheard
When too heavy to sustain they crumble
With a thunder; crawl to a new yard.

Dreams are infectious, parasitic cruel
Their beauty lasts for too long
They bloom on lighthouse towers
Long after fragrances are gone.

They, unlike, the roses of love
Need not thorns to make you bleed
They secrete infectious blood water
From depths of heart and always succeed.

'Buy these dreams and get rid of truth
Dwell in a trance typical of youth'
Thus I sell my demonous dreams
Conspire to kill, promise to sooth.

And when I am done with the buzz of bazaar
I walk slowly to the shelter I seek
The true, pure essence of love, of truth
Eternal beauty, only chosen can keep.

I offer all I earned and more
For a drop to rekindle the lamp of my life
I have been cheated enough I thought
On your altar, my hopes survive.

Imperfect

You
Like an art
Must not
Be perfect.
What I seek
Is what I find
In every gesture
Every word
Every bundle of air
That passes through you
And emerges
Soaked in rainbow
Of five colours
Twisted like a smile,
Brimming
Without waiting
For sky
Or sun
Or water...
I love this urgency.
Denial

And beauty
Smudged
Smoked
Skewed
Serene
Imperfectly true!

Pact

Meet me
Guarded by dead of night
Treading on dreams
Unseen
Burying them
With your gravity.

Meet me
Break a promise
Fill a part
Of your play
Commit the theft
Of deadly desires
Consume them.

Dissolve
Burn in a pyre
We won't remember it
Whenever we meet
And we won't forget
Whenever we don't.

Peace

If there was
A river of peace
It washed our feet
And flew away
Splashes died
On hot rocks
Of life
Traces in eyes
I threw away.

If it was
It was in a moment
That passed
Forever
I knew that day.

If You Ever Love

If you ever love
Love always
Don't love on your terms
Not in perpetual gaze
Don't love as a darling
Forgotten beyond the chase.

Love as moon of desert
Love as midnight sun
Love as shades of laughter
Love as work undone.

Love as dream of a dreamer
Love as worship of art
Love as kill of a glory
Love as a path to chart.

Love as anything but chance
Beyond the words 'what if'
Love as a wild, wild sailor
Ready to find or miss.

Love as wind of winters
No perfect flowery ways
Love as a free bird of summer
Not a slave of length of days.

Love if not to the brim
Love, if not so chaste
Love not as to prove love
Love not as ritual or haste.

Don't love as the gods do
In heavenly bliss and grace
Love a love imperfect
But let it be
Always.

Healer

I know more than nothing
Of windows and souls
To call your eyes
A window to my soul.

I need more than emptiness
To peep inside me
And doors and windows
Are aberrations
Glorified vacuums,
Pathways of chaos,
Leakages; unwanted air.

You can't claim
To behold
That window in you,
Destroying
The castles I guarded
By mere air.

Book of Life

Bloom a delicate poppy
In the graveyard on balcony
Let it gaze the stars, the sky
And sleep in lazy harmony
Talk to the wind, the children
Laugh in the melody of air
Walk without a burden
Dream without any care.

Rip a page a day
From the book of life
Ignorant of what's gone
Uncertain what arrives.

Rip with care
For ink may spill
Blood flows in the veins
Of some words
Let pages fly
In abyss of past
Anticipate in

Prime of youth
Fear as an old shark.

Who knows who writes?
Who knows which part?

Masters came in chain
Chained hands
Ventured in dark
Read the unwritten
Before you are in charge
Tears, dust, fragrance
Colour, age, flowers
Language of a master art.

Rip what you know
And not; rip it apart
Teach life for once
To slip in grace
From dawn to a setting heart.

Conversation

You have grown too quickly
Despite yourself
Forgetting so easily
As if a habit
Has consumed your
Old fatigued brain.

Too wise to laugh
Or cry with me.

Reminds me
Of the old advisor,
Wise nodding head
Whom no one ever knew
Was deaf
Till she died.

You remind me suddenly
Of many things
Frail weak and grey
Still grand

Majestic
Though withering
Time has defeated you
Too soon
And too easily.

I am battling this long darkness
In the blink of my eyes
And you are drinking
The dripping redness of clouds
Outgrowing your shadow
Even in a setting sun.

You have sadly
Grown too quickly
To be identified
Or remembered
Any more.

Said the mirror
Before I shattered it.

Scribbling

I am God again tonight
My arms are time
And I shift them
As and when I wish.

Erasing words
With a swipe of a finger
Moving to a new time.

Trying to remember
Who I was
Before I erased myself
From your words
In my phone.

Prisoner of Dark

Night
Captures you
Executes me
Tortures dreams
Spares mystery
Kills my light
Sprouts dark side
Slowly stealthily
It converts me.

I grow to fight
For your trace in me
But die
Each night
In its custody
I am the moon
You, my sun

That's why
I die
When you look away
Reborn
As you look at me.

Everlasting

Everlasting songs of glee
Float in
Arms of night
Carry the burden of dreams
To a land
So out of sight.

Everlasting fragrances lonely
Wander in pastures
With fright
Slowly sprinkle a memory
Of love laden
Days so
Bright.

Everlasting stories of yearnings
Of that
Not true false
Wrong or right
Not near nor departed
Unfold
Only in twilight.

Struggle

What does one think of?
When night whispers to darkness
And none surrenders to the other
Parallel, undissolved
Dripping pieces of each,
Unresolved.

What does one think of?
When words fight with mind
And none defeats the other
Ferocious, pretended
Struggle seeping endlessly
Undefended.

What does one think of?
When actions encounter destiny
And none identifies the other
Betrayed, belittled
Dragging each other's sorrows
Unsettled.

Time

To flow or to grow
Rooted or eroding
Sweeping past what all was
Or flourishing in static embrace
An eternal dilemma of time.

To destroy or be crushed
Intoxication of control
Or pleasure of submission
To chase a younger shadow
Yet to born
Or cry over the withering
Dying oneself?

To soak in
The sorrows, solitude
Or to bear
Illusions of belonging?
An eternal dilemma of time.

To paint on the fingers
Of a slipping day
Or be carved upon
By cruel stories,
To be hidden or not
To slide down or choose to stay
In sand of an hourglass
An eternal dilemma of time.

A Shadow of Memories

To bloom, wither, die
Is destiny
Of love, life, truth.

To take roots
Like a wild flower,
An accident
Of insignificance.

Growing to become,
Is fallacy of all.

Proclaims the shadow
Emerging tall.

From where not light
Nor darkness speaks

Tripti Bhatt

What was? Before,
deaths of flickering moments
What remains now
Not crooked, lame or defeated?

The lighthouses have crumbled
Fallen prey to impermanence
Mortal dreams
Lost in the ocean of time.

All peripheral
Illusive, temporary
Has grown to defy endings.

Dissolving calmly
Into and alike
A shadow of memories.

Not Beautiful

Silences apart
For a love to depart
It was not
A beautiful day
The streams of sorrow
Meander in deserts
A false tomorrow
Loneliness treasures.

I hoped I would
Be trapped not
Like hot chocolate
Seeped in dry crevices
As the vapours
End the short romance
I realize
With ashes to dance
It was not
A beautiful day.

Trap me or kill
Talk or smile still
A weird warmth
Two great divides
And a long day
To bear
How do I drag
Emptiness and
Hope together?

Serenity
Wrapped in thunder
A delicate lost melody
For my heart suffices
To empty it merciless
Or to choke to brim
But to do both
To an innocent love
It was not
A beautiful day.

Reader

Some are remembered
In sculptures
Some in philosophy
Some brutally forgotten
Guardians of mystery.

Don't open those doors
Of my words
For an avalanche
Controls itself in recluse
How else would it
Cherish
Forbidden history.

Grey pavement exists
Across time and space
To walk to run to read
Is to remind
The foolish ways of grace.

Euthanasia

Will you kill me
With weapons divine
Such that I be dead
Only through you?

Take a new form,
Enter a new world
Never be again
What I was,
Never look back
To pain or its cause!

Will you kill me
And thus
Create?

Will you love me
In your wrath?

Can I dive
In a new world

Still be hanging
Through a thread
Of your command?

Can you drop ink
On blank pages of destiny
Can you decide?
Does your shrewdness
Morph enough?
Can I remember
Which was my side?

Can you kill me
So that I be made
Again, fresh, unspoilt
Unfazed?

Can you create
A grief vast,
Yet profound?
In that ocean
Of pain
Can the last smile
Be mine?
Can you kill me
With weapons divine?

Acidic

Acid of time
Burns me
Not to disfigure
But to renew
Allows me to die
Selectively
And shine again
Till I crave
Suffocated with
Too much of the world
For another shot
Of a new skin
A birth borrowed
And you
Loyally
Burn your charm
Hypnotic agelessness
Store it in a bottle
Ready to kill
Not knowing

When death
Will deny
New debts
Nor when
This cocktail
Of love and more
Will consume
All of us.

Forever

Will you be forever
If forever is a day
And forget old promises
Let torrents wash clay.

Start afresh forever anew
With the calm of dawn
Throw the worldly baggage
Live a life withdrawn?

Will you smell the daisies
Inside a shell of past
Laugh, sing aloud afar
Till the madness last?

Will you console my storms
Quench the shrewd fire?
Will the darkness sink
In words of a playful liar?

Will you or will not
Question my presence?
Will the look be frivolous
Yet imprint intense?

Will you break promises
Like promise is a farce?
Will you worship the gods
Hiding in these towers?

Light a lamp of memory
As you fade away
Forever is ultimately
Just a beautiful day.

River in Moonlight

I run
Like a serpent
Curvaceous
All night
Washed
By droplets
Of your
Flickering light.

I carry the
Softness
Of stories
By my side
I crave for
Plucking
The stars
From night.

I smile
At dusty
Remnants
Of pride
I wash
All tired
Dreams
From your side.

Parallel
I trace
Your journeys
Midnight
Alone I watch
Your surrender
To a might.

Too deep
I have been
To absorb
This suicide
What was
What will be
Is all
Out of sight.

Mysterious
My ways
To lure
You inside
Invite to
This world
Of depths
Of height.

There were
There are
Glories
To preside
I was
I am,
Just
A river
In moonlight.